Awakened

2 *Gratitude*

A day & night reflective journal to
encourage mindfulness, self-care,
affirmation, and positivity.

Larissa H. Rhone

This Journal Belongs To

_____

Awakened 2 Gratitude: Gratitude Journal
Copyright © 2021 by Journey 2 Free Publishing.

ISBN - 978-1-954553-13-2

What is gratitude?

gra-ti-tude: noun - the quality of being thankful; readiness to show appreciation for and return kindness.

Gratitude is Everything! Gratitude is acknowledging all that is good, all that you already have, and being appreciative for all the simple blessings that encompass you. Set the precedence for each day, use this journal and make it a daily habit of reflecting on things great or small that you are thankful for. Reflect and record - a simple breath, a smell, taste, an act of kindness, a breath-taking view - Be intentional, take a few minutes, sit in silence and pen your way into cultivating an attitude of gratitude and uncover joy, peace, and contentment in your hearts, minds, and lives.

Hey Seeker,

Gratitude is Everything! Giving thanks and being appreciative seems a natural thing to do and be, however for a lot of people, this is not true. In spite of how we try, life happens. Some days are good, some days bad, and some days we can barely make it, though. And yes, while some things are beyond our control, there is something we can do. We can choose how to respond to and how we will be affected by our daily challenges.

We can choose to be intentional, alter the way we think, and develop a healthy habit of focusing on the positive, be it great or small. It doesn't matter if you are a chronic complainer, that struggles to find the simple joy's in your every day, or if, like me, for years battle with anxiety, depression, and insecurity that drained my energy, clouded my rationale, and overpowered my decision-making ability. I got tired of wallowing in self-pity, realizing that the' woo is me' mentality kept me from tapping into The Who I desired to be. I grew weary; I needed an awakening. After some deep soul searching, I began making some subtle shifts, focusing my attention on some simple but easily overlooked blessings I took for granted – the ability to move my fingers, arms, legs, a warm place to sleep, my children's smile, the smell of petrichor when it rains, the sunlight on the smell of petrichor when it rains, the sunlight on my face, talking with a friend, hugging my nieces and nephew, it's the simple things that mean the most.

Join me on this journey; take a few moments each day and evening to record:

- Your Mood
- An Affirmation
- Three things you are grateful for.
- Three People you are thankful for.
- Three Things you are looking forward to
- A boundary you set for yourself...

Awaken 2 Gratitude - Invest some time in cultivating an attitude of gratitude and watch your life change for the better. Join me; let's take this journey together. Happy journaling. From my heart to yours. Larissa.

Daily Gratitude

Date: _____   Time: _____

My mood right now...

_____

_____

I am grateful for

1. _____
2. _____
3. _____

Today's Affirmation

I am _____

_____

_____

_____

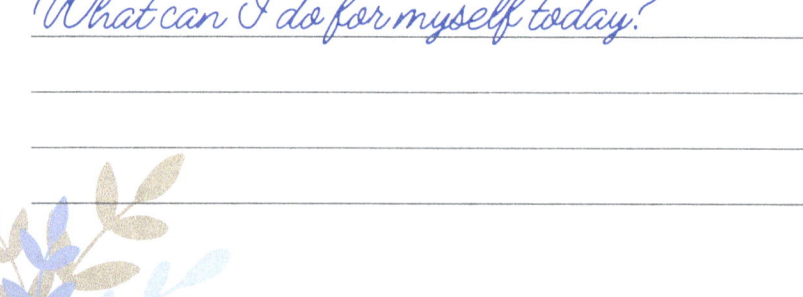

I am looking forward to...

_____

_____

_____

What can I do for myself today?

_____

_____

_____

Evening Gratitude

Date: _____   Time: _____

What caused me anxiety today?

_____

_____

_____

What did I do for myself today, and what did I say No/Yes to?

_____

_____

What boundaries did I set?

_____

_____

_____

_____

My mood right now...

_____

_____

Affirmation:

I am grateful that today...

_____

_____

_____

_____

_____

_____

Daily Gratitude

Date: _____   Time: _____

My mood right now...

_____

_____

I am grateful for

1 _____

2 _____

3 _____

Today's Affirmation

I am _____

_____

_____

_____

I am looking forward to...

_____

_____

_____

What can I do for myself today?

_____

_____

_____

Evening Gratitude

Date: _____   Time: _____

What caused me anxiety today?

_____
_____
_____

What did I do for myself today, and what did I say No/Yes to?

_____
_____

What boundaries did I set?

_____
_____
_____

My mood right now...

_____
_____

Affirmation: _____

I am grateful that today...

_____
_____
_____
_____
_____
_____

Daily Gratitude

Date: _____   Time: _____

My mood right now...
_____

_____

I am grateful for

1 _____

2 _____

3 _____

Today's Affirmation

I am _____

_____

_____

_____

I am looking forward to...
_____

_____

_____

What can I do for myself today?
_____

_____

_____

_____

Evening Gratitude

Date: _____   Time: _____

What caused me anxiety today?

_____

_____

_____

What did I do for myself today,
and what did I say No / Yes to?

_____

_____

What boundaries did I set?

_____

_____

_____

My mood right now...

_____

_____

Affirmation:

I am grateful that today...

_____

_____

_____

_____

_____

Daily Gratitude

Date: _____   Time: _____

My mood right now...
_____
_____

I am grateful for

1 _____

2 _____

3 _____

Today's Affirmation

I am _____
_____
_____
_____

I am looking forward to...
_____
_____
_____

What can I do for myself today?
_____
_____
_____

Evening Gratitude

Date: _____   Time: _____

What caused me anxiety today?

_____

_____

_____

What did I do for myself today, and what did I say No/Yes to?

_____

_____

What boundaries did I set?

_____

_____

_____

My mood right now...

_____

_____

Affirmation: _____

I am grateful that today...

_____

_____

_____

_____

_____

_____

Daily Gratitude

Date: _____   Time: _____

My mood right now...
_____
_____

I am grateful for

1 _____
2 _____
3 _____

Today's Affirmation

I am _____
_____
_____
_____

I am looking forward to...
_____
_____
_____

What can I do for myself today?
_____
_____
_____

Evening Gratitude

Date: _____

Time: _____

What caused me anxiety today?

_____

_____

_____

What did I do for myself today, and what did I say No/Yes to?

_____

_____

What boundaries did I set?

_____

_____

_____

My mood right now...

_____

_____

Affirmation:

I am grateful that today...

_____

_____

_____

_____

_____

Daily Gratitude

Date: _____   Time: _____

My mood right now...

_____

_____

I am grateful for

1 _____

2 _____

3 _____

Today's Affirmation

I am _____

_____

_____

_____

I am looking forward to...

_____

_____

_____

What can I do for myself today?

_____

_____

_____

Evening Gratitude

Date: _____   Time: _____

What caused me anxiety today?

_____
_____
_____

What did I do for myself today,
and what did I say No/ Yes to?

_____
_____
_____

What boundaries did I set?

_____
_____
_____
_____

My mood right now...

_____
_____

Affirmation:

I am grateful that today...

_____
_____
_____
_____
_____
_____

Daily Gratitude

Date: _____   Time: _____

My mood right now...

_____

I am grateful for

1 _____

2 _____

3 _____

Today's Affirmation

I am _____

_____

_____

_____

I am looking forward to...

_____

_____

_____

What can I do for myself today?

_____

_____

_____

Evening Gratitude

Date: _____   Time: _____

What caused me anxiety today?

_____
_____
_____
_____

What did I do for myself today, and what did I say No/Yes to?

_____
_____
_____

What boundaries did I set?

_____
_____
_____
_____

My mood right now...

_____
_____

Affirmation:

I am grateful that today...

_____
_____
_____
_____
_____
_____

Daily Gratitude

Date: _____   Time: _____

My mood right now...

_____

_____

I am grateful for

1 _____

2 _____

3 _____

Today's Affirmation

I am _____

_____

_____

_____

I am looking forward to...

_____

_____

_____

What can I do for myself today?

_____

_____

_____

Evening Gratitude

Date: _____   Time: _____

What caused me anxiety today?
_____
_____
_____

What did I do for myself today,
and what did I say No/ Yes to?
_____
_____

What boundaries did I set?
_____
_____
_____

My mood right now...
_____
_____

Affirmation:
_____

I am grateful that today...
_____
_____
_____
_____
_____
_____

Daily Gratitude

Date: _____   Time: _____

My mood right now...

_____

_____

I am grateful for

1 _____

2 _____

3 _____

Today's Affirmation

I am _____

_____

_____

_____

I am looking forward to...

_____

_____

_____

_____

What can I do for myself today?

_____

_____

_____

_____

Evening Gratitude

Date: _____   Time: _____

What caused me anxiety today? _____
_____
_____

What did I do for myself today,
and what did I say No/ Yes to?
_____
_____

What boundaries did I set?
_____
_____
_____
_____

My mood right now...
_____
_____

Affirmation: _____

I am grateful that today... _____
_____
_____
_____
_____

Daily Gratitude

Date: _____   Time: _____

My mood right now...
_____
_____

I am grateful for

1 _____
2 _____
3 _____

Today's Affirmation

I am _____
_____
_____
_____

I am looking forward to...
_____
_____
_____

What can I do for myself today?
_____
_____
_____
_____

Evening Gratitude

Date: _____   Time: _____

What caused me anxiety today?

_____

_____

What did I do for myself today, and what did I say No/Yes to?

_____

_____

What boundaries did I set?

_____

_____

_____

_____

My mood right now...

_____

_____

Affirmation:

_____

I am grateful that today...

_____

_____

_____

_____

_____

Daily Gratitude

Date: _____   Time: _____

My mood right now...
_____
_____

I am grateful for

1 _____
2 _____
3 _____

Today's Affirmation

I am _____
_____
_____
_____

I am looking forward to...
_____
_____
_____

What can I do for myself today?
_____
_____
_____

Evening Gratitude

Date: _____   Time: _____

What caused me anxiety today?

_____
_____
_____

What did I do for myself today, and what did I say No/Yes to?

_____
_____

What boundaries did I set?

_____
_____
_____
_____

My mood right now...

_____
_____

Affirmation:

I am grateful that today...

_____
_____
_____
_____
_____
_____

Daily Gratitude

Date: _____   Time: _____

My mood right now...
_____
_____

I am grateful for

1 _____

2 _____

3 _____

Today's Affirmation

I am _____
_____
_____
_____

I am looking forward to...
_____
_____
_____

What can I do for myself today?
_____
_____
_____

Evening Gratitude

Date: _____

Time: _____

What caused me anxiety today?

_____

_____

What did I do for myself today,
and what did I say No/Yes to?

_____

_____

What boundaries did I set?

_____

_____

_____

My mood right now...

_____

_____

Affirmation:

I am grateful that today...

_____

_____

_____

_____

_____

Daily Gratitude

Date: _____   Time: _____

My mood right now...
_____
_____

I am grateful for

1 _____
2 _____
3 _____

Today's Affirmation

I am _____
_____
_____
_____

I am looking forward to...
_____
_____
_____

What can I do for myself today?
_____
_____
_____

Evening Gratitude

Date: _____   Time: _____

What caused me anxiety today?

_____

_____

_____

What did I do for myself today, and what did I say No/ Yes to?

_____

_____

_____

What boundaries did I set?

_____

_____

_____

_____

My mood right now...

_____

_____

_____

Affirmation: _____

I am grateful that today...

_____

_____

_____

_____

_____

_____

Daily Gratitude

Date: _____   Time: _____

My mood right now...

_____

_____

I am grateful for

1 _____

2 _____

3 _____

Today's Affirmation

I am _____

_____

_____

_____

I am looking forward to...

_____

_____

_____

What can I do for myself today?

_____

_____

_____

Evening Gratitude

Date: _____   Time: _____

What caused me anxiety today?

_____

_____

_____

What did I do for myself today,
and what did I say No/Yes to?

_____

_____

What boundaries did I set?

_____

_____

_____

_____

My mood right now...

_____

_____

Affirmation: _____

I am grateful that today...

_____

_____

_____

_____

_____

_____

Daily Gratitude

Date: _____

Time: _____

My mood right now...

_____

_____

I am grateful for

1 _____

2 _____

3 _____

Today's Affirmation

I am _____

_____

_____

_____

I am looking forward to...

_____

_____

_____

_____

What can I do for myself today?

_____

_____

_____

_____

Evening Gratitude

Date: _____   Time: _____

What caused me anxiety today?

_____

_____

What did I do for myself today,
and what did I say No/Yes to?

_____

_____

What boundaries did I set?

_____

_____

_____

_____

My mood right now...

_____

_____

Affirmation: _____

I am grateful that today...

_____

_____

_____

_____

_____

_____

Daily Gratitude

Date: _____   Time: _____

My mood right now...

_____

_____

I am grateful for

1 _____

2 _____

3 _____

Today's Affirmation

I am _____

_____

_____

_____

I am looking forward to...

_____

_____

_____

What can I do for myself today?

_____

_____

_____

_____

Evening Gratitude

Date: _____ Time: _____

What caused me anxiety today?

_____
_____
_____

What did I do for myself today, and what did I say No/Yes to?

_____
_____

What boundaries did I set?

_____
_____
_____
_____

My mood right now...

_____
_____

Affirmation: _____

I am grateful that today...

_____
_____
_____
_____
_____
_____
_____

Daily Gratitude

Date: _____   Time: _____

My mood right now...

_____

_____

I am grateful for

1 _____

2 _____

3 _____

Today's Affirmation

I am _____

_____

_____

_____

I am looking forward to...

_____

_____

_____

What can I do for myself today?

_____

_____

_____

Evening Gratitude

Date: _____   Time: _____

What caused me anxiety today?

_____
_____

What did I do for myself today,
and what did I say No/Yes to?

_____
_____

What boundaries did I set?

_____
_____
_____
_____

My mood right now...

_____
_____

Affirmation:

I am grateful that today...

_____
_____
_____
_____
_____
_____

Daily Gratitude

Date: _____   Time: _____

My mood right now...
_____
_____

I am grateful for

1 _____
2 _____
3 _____

Today's Affirmation

I am _____
_____
_____
_____

I am looking forward to...
_____
_____
_____

What can I do for myself today?
_____
_____
_____

Evening Gratitude

Date: _____ Time: _____

What caused me anxiety today?

_____
_____
_____

What did I do for myself today,
and what did I say No/Yes to?

_____
_____
_____

What boundaries did I set?

_____
_____
_____
_____

My mood right now...

_____
_____

Affirmation:

I am grateful that today...

_____
_____
_____
_____
_____
_____

Daily Gratitude

Date: _____   Time: _____

My mood right now...
_____
_____

I am grateful for

1 _____
2 _____
3 _____

Today's Affirmation

I am _____
_____
_____
_____

I am looking forward to...
_____
_____
_____

What can I do for myself today?
_____
_____
_____

Evening Gratitude

Date: _____ Time: _____

What caused me anxiety today?

_____
_____
_____

What did I do for myself today, and what did I say No/ Yes to?

_____
_____
_____

What boundaries did I set?

_____
_____
_____
_____

My mood right now...

_____
_____

Affirmation:

I am grateful that today...

_____
_____
_____
_____
_____
_____

Daily Gratitude

Date: _____   Time: _____

My mood right now...

_____

_____

I am grateful for

1 _____

2 _____

3 _____

Today's Affirmation

I am _____

_____

_____

_____

I am looking forward to...

_____

_____

_____

What can I do for myself today?

_____

_____

_____

Evening Gratitude

Date: _____

Time: _____

What caused me anxiety today?

_____
_____
_____

What did I do for myself today, and what did I say No/Yes to?

_____
_____

What boundaries did I set?

_____
_____
_____
_____

My mood right now...

_____
_____

Affirmation:

I am grateful that today...

_____
_____
_____
_____
_____
_____

Daily Gratitude

Date: _____   Time: _____

My mood right now...

_____

_____

I am grateful for

1 _____

2 _____

3 _____

Today's Affirmation

I am _____

_____

_____

_____

I am looking forward to...

_____

_____

_____

What can I do for myself today?

_____

_____

_____

_____

Evening Gratitude

Date: _____   Time: _____

What caused me anxiety today?

_____

_____

_____

What did I do for myself today,
and what did I say No/Yes to?

_____

_____

What boundaries did I set?

_____

_____

_____

_____

My mood right now...

_____

_____

Affirmation:

I am grateful that today...

_____

_____

_____

_____

_____

_____

Daily Gratitude

Date: _____   Time: _____

My mood right now...
_____
_____

I am grateful for

1 _____
2 _____
3 _____

Today's Affirmation

I am _____
_____
_____
_____

I am looking forward to...
_____
_____
_____

What can I do for myself today?
_____
_____
_____

Evening Gratitude

Date: _____

Time: _____

What caused me anxiety today?

_____

_____

What did I do for myself today,
and what did I say No/Yes to?

_____

_____

What boundaries did I set?

_____

_____

_____

My mood right now...

_____

_____

Affirmation:

I am grateful that today...

_____

_____

_____

_____

_____

Daily Gratitude

Date: _____   Time: _____

My mood right now...

_____
_____

I am grateful for

1 _____
2 _____
3 _____

Today's Affirmation

I am _____
_____
_____
_____

I am looking forward to...

_____
_____
_____

What can I do for myself today?

_____
_____
_____

Evening Gratitude

Date: _____   Time: _____

What caused me anxiety today?

_____

_____

_____

What did I do for myself today,
and what did I say No/ Yes to?

_____

_____

What boundaries did I set?

_____

_____

_____

My mood right now...

_____

_____

Affirmation:

I am grateful that today...

_____

_____

_____

_____

_____

Daily Gratitude

Date: _____ Time: _____

My mood right now...
_____
_____

I am grateful for

1 _____
2 _____
3 _____

Today's Affirmation

I am _____
_____
_____
_____

I am looking forward to...
_____
_____
_____

What can I do for myself today?
_____
_____
_____
_____

Evening Gratitude

Date: _____   Time: _____

What caused me anxiety today?

_____

_____

What did I do for myself today, and what did I say No/Yes to?

_____

_____

What boundaries did I set?

_____

_____

My mood right now...

_____

_____

Affirmation: _____

I am grateful that today...

_____

_____

_____

_____

_____

Daily Gratitude

Date: _____   Time: _____

My mood right now...
_____
_____

I am grateful for

1 _____
2 _____
3 _____

Today's Affirmation

I am _____
_____
_____
_____

I am looking forward to...
_____
_____
_____

What can I do for myself today?
_____
_____
_____

Evening Gratitude

Date: _____   Time: _____

What caused me anxiety today?
_____
_____
_____

What did I do for myself today,
and what did I say No/ Yes to?
_____
_____

What boundaries did I set?
_____
_____
_____

My mood right now...
_____
_____

Affirmation:
_____

I am grateful that today...
_____
_____
_____
_____
_____
_____

Daily Gratitude

Date: _____   Time: _____

My mood right now...
_____
_____

I am grateful for

1 _____
2 _____
3 _____

Today's Affirmation

I am _____
_____
_____
_____

I am looking forward to...
_____
_____
_____

What can I do for myself today?
_____
_____
_____

Evening Gratitude

Date: _____   Time: _____

What caused me anxiety today?

_____

_____

What did I do for myself today,
and what did I say No/Yes to?

_____

_____

What boundaries did I set?

_____

_____

_____

_____

My mood right now...

_____

_____

Affirmation:

I am grateful that today...

_____

_____

_____

_____

_____

Daily Gratitude

Date: _____   Time: _____

My mood right now...
_____
_____

I am grateful for

1 _____
2 _____
3 _____

Today's Affirmation

I am _____
_____
_____
_____

I am looking forward to...
_____
_____
_____

What can I do for myself today?
_____
_____
_____

Evening Gratitude

Date: _____   Time: _____

What caused me anxiety today?

_____

_____

_____

What did I do for myself today,
and what did I say No/ Yes to?

_____

_____

What boundaries did I set?

_____

_____

_____

_____

My mood right now...

_____

_____

Affirmation:

I am grateful that today...

_____

_____

_____

_____

_____

_____

Daily Gratitude

Date: _____   Time: _____

My mood right now...
_____
_____

I am grateful for
1 _____
2 _____
3 _____

Today's Affirmation

I am _____
_____
_____
_____

I am looking forward to...
_____
_____
_____

What can I do for myself today?
_____
_____
_____
_____

Evening Gratitude

Date: _____   Time: _____

What caused me anxiety today?

_____

_____

What did I do for myself today, and what did I say No/ Yes to?

_____

_____

What boundaries did I set?

_____

_____

_____

My mood right now...

_____

_____

Affirmation:

I am grateful that today...

_____

_____

_____

_____

_____

_____

Daily Gratitude

Date: _____   Time: _____

My mood right now...
_____
_____

I am grateful for

1 _____
2 _____
3 _____

Today's Affirmation

I am _____
_____
_____
_____

I am looking forward to...
_____
_____
_____

What can I do for myself today?
_____
_____
_____

Evening Gratitude

Date: _____   Time: _____

What caused me anxiety today?

_____

_____

_____

What did I do for myself today,
and what did I say No/ Yes to?

_____

_____

_____

What boundaries did I set?

_____

_____

_____

_____

My mood right now...

_____

_____

Affirmation:

I am grateful that today...

_____

_____

_____

_____

_____

_____

Daily Gratitude

Date: _____   Time: _____

My mood right now...
_____
_____

I am grateful for

1 _____
2 _____
3 _____

Today's Affirmation

I am _____
_____
_____
_____

I am looking forward to...
_____
_____
_____

What can I do for myself today?
_____
_____
_____

Evening Gratitude

Date: _____   Time: _____

What caused me anxiety today?

_____

_____

_____

What did I do for myself today,
and what did I say No/Yes to?

_____

_____

_____

What boundaries did I set?

_____

_____

_____

_____

My mood right now...

_____

_____

Affirmation:

I am grateful that today...

_____

_____

_____

_____

_____

Daily Gratitude

Date: _____   Time: _____

My mood right now...
_____
_____

I am grateful for

1 _____
2 _____
3 _____

Today's Affirmation

I am _____
_____
_____
_____

I am looking forward to...
_____
_____
_____

What can I do for myself today?
_____
_____
_____
_____

Evening Gratitude

Date: _____   Time: _____

What caused me anxiety today?

_____

_____

_____

What did I do for myself today, and what did I say No/Yes to?

_____

_____

What boundaries did I set?

_____

_____

_____

My mood right now...

_____

_____

Affirmation:

I am grateful that today...

_____

_____

_____

_____

_____

_____

Daily Gratitude

Date: _____   Time: _____

My mood right now...
_____
_____

I am grateful for

1 _____
2 _____
3 _____

Today's Affirmation

I am _____
_____
_____
_____

I am looking forward to...
_____
_____
_____

What can I do for myself today?
_____
_____
_____

Evening Gratitude

Date: _____

Time: _____

What caused me anxiety today?

_____

_____

_____

What did I do for myself today,
and what did I say No/Yes to?

_____

_____

_____

What boundaries did I set?

_____

_____

_____

_____

My mood right now...

_____

_____

Affirmation:

I am grateful that today...

_____

_____

_____

_____

_____

_____

Daily Gratitude

Date: _____   Time: _____

My mood right now...
_____

I am grateful for

1 _____

2 _____

3 _____

Today's Affirmation

I am _____
_____
_____
_____

I am looking forward to...
_____
_____
_____

What can I do for myself today?
_____
_____
_____

Evening Gratitude

Date: _____   Time: _____

What caused me anxiety today?

_____

_____

_____

What did I do for myself today, and what did I say No/Yes to?

_____

_____

_____

What boundaries did I set?

_____

_____

_____

My mood right now...

_____

_____

Affirmation:

_____

I am grateful that today...

_____

_____

_____

_____

_____

Daily Gratitude

Date: _____   Time: _____

My mood right now...
_____
_____

I am grateful for

1 _____
2 _____
3 _____

Today's Affirmation

I am _____
_____
_____
_____

I am looking forward to...
_____
_____
_____

What can I do for myself today?
_____
_____
_____
_____

Evening Gratitude

Date: _____   Time: _____

What caused me anxiety today?

_____
_____
_____

What did I do for myself today, and what did I say No/Yes to?

_____
_____
_____

What boundaries did I set?

_____
_____
_____
_____

My mood right now...

_____
_____

Affirmation: _____

I am grateful that today...

_____
_____
_____
_____
_____
_____

Daily Gratitude

Date: _____   Time: _____

My mood right now...
_____
_____

I am grateful for

1 _____
2 _____
3 _____

Today's Affirmation

I am _____
_____
_____
_____

I am looking forward to...
_____
_____
_____

What can I do for myself today?
_____
_____
_____

Evening Gratitude

Date: _____   Time: _____

What caused me anxiety today?

_____

_____

_____

What did I do for myself today, and what did I say No/Yes to?

_____

_____

What boundaries did I set?

_____

_____

_____

_____

My mood right now...

_____

_____

Affirmation:

I am grateful that today...

_____

_____

_____

_____

_____

_____

Daily Gratitude

Date: _____   Time: _____

My mood right now...
_____
_____

I am grateful for

1 _____

2 _____

3 _____

Today's Affirmation

I am _____
_____
_____
_____

I am looking forward to...
_____
_____
_____

What can I do for myself today?
_____
_____
_____
_____

Evening Gratitude

Date: _____   Time: _____

What caused me anxiety today?

_____
_____
_____

What did I do for myself today,
and what did I say No/Yes to?

_____
_____

What boundaries did I set?

_____
_____
_____
_____

My mood right now...

_____
_____

Affirmation:

I am grateful that today...

_____
_____
_____
_____
_____
_____

Daily Gratitude

Date: _____   Time: _____

My mood right now...
_____
_____

I am grateful for

1 _____

2 _____

3 _____

Today's Affirmation

I am _____
_____
_____
_____

I am looking forward to...
_____
_____
_____

What can I do for myself today?
_____
_____
_____

Evening Gratitude

Date: _____   Time: _____

What caused me anxiety today?

_____

_____

_____

What did I do for myself today, and what did I say No/Yes to?

_____

_____

What boundaries did I set?

_____

_____

_____

My mood right now...

_____

_____

Affirmation: _____

I am grateful that today...

_____

_____

_____

_____

_____

_____

Daily Gratitude

Date: _____   Time: _____

My mood right now...

_____
_____

I am grateful for

1 _____

2 _____

3 _____

Today's Affirmation

I am _____
_____
_____
_____

I am looking forward to...

_____
_____
_____

What can I do for myself today?

_____
_____
_____

Evening Gratitude

Date: _____   Time: _____

What caused me anxiety today?
_____
_____
_____

What did I do for myself today,
and what did I say No/Yes to?
_____
_____

What boundaries did I set?
_____
_____
_____
_____

My mood right now...
_____
_____

Affirmation:

I am grateful that today...
_____
_____
_____
_____
_____
_____

Daily Gratitude

Date: _____   Time: _____

My mood right now...
_____
_____

I am grateful for

1 _____
2 _____
3 _____

Today's Affirmation

I am _____
_____
_____
_____

I am looking forward to...
_____
_____
_____

What can I do for myself today?
_____
_____
_____

Evening Gratitude

Date: _____ Time: _____

What caused me anxiety today?

_____

_____

_____

What did I do for myself today,
and what did I say No/Yes to?

_____

_____

What boundaries did I set?

_____

_____

_____

My mood right now...

_____

_____

Affirmation:

I am grateful that today...

_____

_____

_____

_____

_____

Daily Gratitude

Date: _____   Time: _____

My mood right now...

_____

_____

I am grateful for

1 _____

2 _____

3 _____

Today's Affirmation

I am _____

_____

_____

_____

I am looking forward to...

_____

_____

_____

What can I do for myself today?

_____

_____

_____

_____

Evening Gratitude

Date: _____   Time: _____

What caused me anxiety today?

_____

_____

What did I do for myself today,
and what did I say No/Yes to?

_____

_____

What boundaries did I set?

_____

_____

_____

_____

My mood right now...

_____

_____

Affirmation:

I am grateful that today...

_____

_____

_____

_____

_____

_____

Daily Gratitude

Date: _____   Time: _____

My mood right now...

_____

_____

I am grateful for

1 _____

2 _____

3 _____

Today's Affirmation

I am _____

_____

_____

_____

I am looking forward to...

_____

_____

_____

What can I do for myself today?

_____

_____

_____

Evening Gratitude

Date: _____   Time: _____

What caused me anxiety today?

_____

_____

_____

What did I do for myself today,
and what did I say No/Yes to?

_____

_____

_____

What boundaries did I set?

_____

_____

_____

_____

My mood right now...

_____

_____

_____

Affirmation:

I am grateful that today...

_____

_____

_____

_____

_____

_____

Daily Gratitude

Date: _____   Time: _____

My mood right now...
_____
_____

I am grateful for

1 _____

2 _____

3 _____

Today's Affirmation

I am _____
_____
_____
_____

I am looking forward to...
_____
_____
_____

What can I do for myself today?
_____
_____
_____

Evening Gratitude

Date: _____   Time: _____

What caused me anxiety today?

_____

_____

_____

What did I do for myself today,
and what did I say No/Yes to?

_____

_____

What boundaries did I set?

_____

_____

_____

My mood right now...

_____

_____

Affirmation:

I am grateful that today...

_____

_____

_____

_____

_____

Daily Gratitude

Date: _____   Time: _____

My mood right now...
_____
_____

I am grateful for

1 _____
2 _____
3 _____

Today's Affirmation

I am _____
_____
_____
_____

I am looking forward to...
_____
_____
_____

What can I do for myself today?
_____
_____
_____
_____

Evening Gratitude

Date: _____   Time: _____

What caused me anxiety today?

_____

_____

_____

What did I do for myself today,
and what did I say No/Yes to?

_____

_____

What boundaries did I set?

_____

_____

_____

_____

My mood right now...

_____

_____

Affirmation:

I am grateful that today...

_____

_____

_____

_____

_____

_____

Daily Gratitude

Date: _____   Time: _____

My mood right now...

_____

_____

I am grateful for

1 _____

2 _____

3 _____

Today's Affirmation

I am _____

_____

_____

_____

I am looking forward to...

_____

_____

_____

What can I do for myself today?

_____

_____

_____

Evening Gratitude

Date: _____   Time: _____

What caused me anxiety today?

_____

_____

What did I do for myself today,
and what did I say No/Yes to?

_____

_____

What boundaries did I set?

_____

_____

_____

My mood right now...

_____

_____

Affirmation:

I am grateful that today...

_____

_____

_____

_____

_____

Daily Gratitude

Date: _____   Time: _____

My mood right now...
_____
_____

I am grateful for

1 _____
2 _____
3 _____

Today's Affirmation

I am _____
_____
_____
_____

I am looking forward to...
_____
_____
_____
_____

What can I do for myself today?
_____
_____
_____
_____

Evening Gratitude

Date: _____   Time: _____

What caused me anxiety today?

_____

_____

_____

What did I do for myself today,
and what did I say No / Yes to?

_____

_____

What boundaries did I set?

_____

_____

_____

My mood right now...

_____

Affirmation: _____

I am grateful that today... _____

_____

_____

_____

_____

_____

Daily Gratitude

Date: _____   Time: _____

My mood right now...

_____

_____

I am grateful for

1 _____

2 _____

3 _____

Today's Affirmation

I am _____

_____

_____

_____

I am looking forward to...

_____

_____

_____

What can I do for myself today?

_____

_____

_____

_____

Evening Gratitude

Date: _____ Time: _____

What caused me anxiety today?

_____

_____

_____

What did I do for myself today,
and what did I say No / Yes to?

_____

_____

_____

What boundaries did I set?

_____

_____

_____

_____

My mood right now...

_____

_____

Affirmation:

I am grateful that today...

_____

_____

_____

_____

_____

_____

_____

Daily Gratitude

Date: _____   Time: _____

My mood right now...

_____

_____

I am grateful for

1 _____

2 _____

3 _____

Today's Affirmation

I am _____

_____

_____

_____

I am looking forward to...

_____

_____

_____

_____

What can I do for myself today?

_____

_____

_____

Evening Gratitude

Date: _____   Time: _____

What caused me anxiety today?

_____

_____

_____

What did I do for myself today,
and what did I say No/ Yes to?

_____

_____

What boundaries did I set?

_____

_____

_____

_____

My mood right now...

_____

_____

Affirmation:

I am grateful that today...

_____

_____

_____

_____

_____

Daily Gratitude

Date: _____   Time: _____

My mood right now...

_____

_____

I am grateful for

1 _____

2 _____

3 _____

Today's Affirmation

I am _____

_____

_____

_____

I am looking forward to...

_____

_____

_____

What can I do for myself today?

_____

_____

_____

_____

Evening Gratitude

Date: _____   Time: _____

What caused me anxiety today?

_____
_____
_____

What did I do for myself today,
and what did I say No/ Yes to?

_____
_____

What boundaries did I set?

_____
_____
_____
_____

My mood right now...

_____
_____

Affirmation:

I am grateful that today...

_____
_____
_____
_____
_____
_____

Daily Gratitude

Date: _____   Time: _____

My mood right now...

_____

_____

I am grateful for

1 _____

2 _____

3 _____

Today's Affirmation

I am _____

_____

_____

_____

I am looking forward to...

_____

_____

_____

What can I do for myself today?

_____

_____

_____

Evening Gratitude

Date: _____   Time: _____

What caused me anxiety today?

_____

_____

_____

What did I do for myself today,
and what did I say No/Yes to?

_____

_____

What boundaries did I set?

_____

_____

_____

My mood right now...

_____

_____

Affirmation:

I am grateful that today...

_____

_____

_____

_____

_____

_____

Daily Gratitude

Date: _____   Time: _____

My mood right now...

_____

_____

I am grateful for

1 _____

2 _____

3 _____

Today's Affirmation

I am _____

_____

_____

_____

I am looking forward to...

_____

_____

_____

What can I do for myself today?

_____

_____

_____

Evening Gratitude

Date: _____   Time: _____

What caused me anxiety today?

_____

_____

_____

What did I do for myself today,
and what did I say No/ Yes to?

_____

_____

What boundaries did I set?

_____

_____

_____

_____

My mood right now...

_____

_____

Affirmation:

I am grateful that today...

_____

_____

_____

_____

_____

Daily Gratitude

Date: _____   Time: _____

My mood right now...
_____
_____

I am grateful for

1 _____
2 _____
3 _____

Today's Affirmation

I am _____
_____
_____
_____

I am looking forward to...
_____
_____
_____

What can I do for myself today?
_____
_____
_____
_____

Evening Gratitude

Date: _____ Time: _____

What caused me anxiety today?

_____

_____

_____

What did I do for myself today,
and what did I say No/ Yes to?

_____

_____

What boundaries did I set?

_____

_____

_____

_____

My mood right now...

_____

_____

Affirmation: _____

I am grateful that today...

_____

_____

_____

_____

_____

_____

Daily Gratitude

Date: _____   Time: _____

My mood right now...

_____

_____

I am grateful for

1 _____

2 _____

3 _____

Today's Affirmation

I am _____

_____

_____

_____

I am looking forward to...

_____

_____

_____

What can I do for myself today?

_____

_____

_____

Evening Gratitude

Date: _____   Time: _____

What caused me anxiety today?

_____

_____

_____

What did I do for myself today,
and what did I say No/ Yes to?

_____

_____

_____

What boundaries did I set?

_____

_____

_____

My mood right now...

_____

_____

Affirmation: _____

I am grateful that today... _____

_____

_____

_____

_____

_____

_____

Daily Gratitude

Date: _____   Time: _____

My mood right now...
_____
_____

I am grateful for

1 _____
2 _____
3 _____

Today's Affirmation

I am _____
_____
_____
_____

I am looking forward to...
_____
_____
_____

What can I do for myself today?
_____
_____
_____

Evening Gratitude

Date: _____   Time: _____

What caused me anxiety today?

_____

_____

_____

What did I do for myself today,
and what did I say No/Yes to?

_____

_____

What boundaries did I set?

_____

_____

_____

My mood right now...

_____

_____

Affirmation:

I am grateful that today...

_____

_____

_____

_____

_____

Daily Gratitude

Date: _____   Time: _____

My mood right now...
_____
_____

I am grateful for

1 _____
2 _____
3 _____

Today's Affirmation

I am _____
_____
_____
_____

I am looking forward to...
_____
_____
_____

What can I do for myself today?
_____
_____
_____
_____

Evening Gratitude

Date: _____   Time: _____

What caused me anxiety today?

_____

_____

_____

What did I do for myself today,
and what did I say No/Yes to?

_____

_____

What boundaries did I set?

_____

_____

_____

My mood right now...

_____

_____

Affirmation: _____

I am grateful that today... _____

_____

_____

_____

_____

_____

Daily Gratitude

Date: _____   Time: _____

My mood right now...
_____
_____

I am grateful for

1 _____
2 _____
3 _____

Today's Affirmation

I am _____
_____
_____
_____

I am looking forward to...
_____
_____
_____

What can I do for myself today?
_____
_____
_____

Evening Gratitude

Date: _____   Time: _____

What caused me anxiety today?

_____

_____

_____

What did I do for myself today,
and what did I say No/Yes to?

_____

_____

_____

What boundaries did I set?

_____

_____

_____

_____

My mood right now...

_____

_____

Affirmation:

_____

I am grateful that today...

_____

_____

_____

_____

_____

_____

Daily Gratitude

Date: _____   Time: _____

My mood right now...

_____

_____

I am grateful for

1 _____

2 _____

3 _____

Today's Affirmation

I am _____

_____

_____

_____

I am looking forward to...

_____

_____

_____

What can I do for myself today?

_____

_____

_____

Evening Gratitude

Date: _____   Time: _____

What caused me anxiety today?

_____

_____

_____

What did I do for myself today,
and what did I say No/Yes to?

_____

_____

What boundaries did I set?

_____

_____

_____

My mood right now...

_____

_____

Affirmation:

I am grateful that today...

_____

_____

_____

_____

_____

Daily Gratitude

Date: _____   Time: _____

My mood right now...
_____
_____

I am grateful for

1 _____
2 _____
3 _____

Today's Affirmation

I am _____
_____
_____
_____

I am looking forward to...
_____
_____
_____

What can I do for myself today?
_____
_____
_____

Evening Gratitude

Date: _____   Time: _____

What caused me anxiety today?

_____

_____

_____

What did I do for myself today, and what did I say No/Yes to?

_____

_____

_____

What boundaries did I set?

_____

_____

_____

_____

My mood right now...

_____

_____

Affirmation: _____

I am grateful that today...

_____

_____

_____

_____

_____

_____

Daily Gratitude

Date: _____   Time: _____

My mood right now...

_____

_____

I am grateful for

1 _____

2 _____

3 _____

Today's Affirmation

I am _____

_____

_____

_____

I am looking forward to...

_____

_____

_____

What can I do for myself today?

_____

_____

_____

_____

Evening Gratitude

Date: _____   Time: _____

What caused me anxiety today?

_____

_____

_____

What did I do for myself today, and what did I say No/ Yes to?

_____

_____

_____

What boundaries did I set?

_____

_____

_____

_____

My mood right now...

_____

_____

_____

Affirmation:

_____

I am grateful that today...

_____

_____

_____

_____

_____

_____

Daily Gratitude

Date: _____   Time: _____

My mood right now...
_____
_____

I am grateful for

1 _____

2 _____

3 _____

Today's Affirmation

I am _____
_____
_____
_____

I am looking forward to...
_____
_____
_____

What can I do for myself today?
_____
_____
_____

Evening Gratitude

Date: _____   Time: _____

What caused me anxiety today?

_____

_____

_____

What did I do for myself today, and what did I say No/ Yes to?

_____

_____

What boundaries did I set?

_____

_____

_____

_____

My mood right now...

_____

_____

Affirmation:

I am grateful that today...

_____

_____

_____

_____

_____

_____

Daily Gratitude

Date: _____   Time: _____

My mood right now...
_____
_____

I am grateful for

1 _____
2 _____
3 _____

Today's Affirmation

I am _____
_____
_____
_____

I am looking forward to...
_____
_____
_____

What can I do for myself today?
_____
_____
_____

Evening Gratitude

Date: _____   Time: _____

What caused me anxiety today?

_____

_____

_____

What did I do for myself today, and what did I say No/ Yes to?

_____

_____

_____

What boundaries did I set?

_____

_____

_____

My mood right now...

_____

_____

Affirmation:

I am grateful that today...

_____

_____

_____

_____

_____

_____

Daily Gratitude

Date: _____   Time: _____

My mood right now...

_____

_____

I am grateful for

1 _____

2 _____

3 _____

Today's Affirmation

I am _____

_____

_____

_____

I am looking forward to...

_____

_____

_____

What can I do for myself today?

_____

_____

_____

Evening Gratitude

Date: _____   Time: _____

What caused me anxiety today?

_____

_____

_____

What did I do for myself today,
and what did I say No/ Yes to?

_____

_____

What boundaries did I set?

_____

_____

_____

My mood right now...

_____

_____

Affirmation:

I am grateful that today...

_____

_____

_____

_____

_____

Daily Gratitude

Date: _____   Time: _____

My mood right now...

_____

_____

I am grateful for

1 _____

2 _____

3 _____

Today's Affirmation

I am _____

_____

_____

_____

I am looking forward to...

_____

_____

_____

What can I do for myself today?

_____

_____

_____

Evening Gratitude

Date: _____   Time: _____

What caused me anxiety today?
_____
_____
_____

What did I do for myself today,
and what did I say No/Yes to?
_____
_____

What boundaries did I set?
_____
_____
_____
_____

My mood right now...
_____
_____

Affirmation:
_____

I am grateful that today...
_____
_____
_____
_____
_____

Daily Gratitude

Date: _____   Time: _____

My mood right now...
_____
_____

I am grateful for

1 _____
2 _____
3 _____

Today's Affirmation

_I am_ _____
_____
_____
_____

I am looking forward to...
_____
_____
_____

What can I do for myself today?
_____
_____
_____

Evening Gratitude

Date: _____   Time: _____

What caused me anxiety today?

_____

_____

_____

_____

What did I do for myself today, and what did I say No/ Yes to?

_____

_____

_____

What boundaries did I set?

_____

_____

_____

_____

My mood right now...

_____

_____

Affirmation:

_____

I am grateful that today...

_____

_____

_____

_____

_____

_____

Daily Gratitude

Date: _____   Time: _____

My mood right now...
_____
_____

I am grateful for

1 _____
2 _____
3 _____

Today's Affirmation

I am _____
_____
_____
_____

I am looking forward to...
_____
_____
_____

What can I do for myself today?
_____
_____
_____
_____

Evening Gratitude

Date: _____   Time: _____

What caused me anxiety today?

_____
_____

What did I do for myself today,
and what did I say No/Yes to?

_____
_____

What boundaries did I set?

_____
_____
_____
_____

My mood right now...

_____
_____

Affirmation:
_____

I am grateful that today...

_____
_____
_____
_____
_____
_____

Daily Gratitude

Date: _____

Time: _____

My mood right now...

_____

_____

I am grateful for

1 _____

2 _____

3 _____

Today's Affirmation

I am _____

_____

_____

_____

I am looking forward to...

_____

_____

_____

What can I do for myself today?

_____

_____

_____

Evening Gratitude

Date: _____   Time: _____

What caused me anxiety today?

_____
_____
_____

What did I do for myself today,
and what did I say No/ Yes to?

_____
_____
_____

What boundaries did I set?

_____
_____
_____
_____

My mood right now...

_____
_____
_____

Affirmation:

I am grateful that today...

_____
_____
_____
_____
_____
_____

Daily Gratitude

Date: _____   Time: _____

My mood right now...
_____
_____

I am grateful for

1 _____
2 _____
3 _____

Today's Affirmation

I am _____
_____
_____
_____

I am looking forward to...
_____
_____
_____

What can I do for myself today?
_____
_____
_____

Evening Gratitude

Date: _____   Time: _____

What caused me anxiety today?

_____

_____

_____

What did I do for myself today,
and what did I say No/ Yes to?

_____

_____

_____

What boundaries did I set?

_____

_____

_____

_____

My mood right now...

_____

_____

Affirmation:

I am grateful that today...

_____

_____

_____

_____

_____

_____

Daily Gratitude

Date: _____   Time: _____

My mood right now...
_____
_____

I am grateful for

1 _____
2 _____
3 _____

Today's Affirmation

I am _____
_____
_____
_____

I am looking forward to...
_____
_____
_____
_____

What can I do for myself today?
_____
_____
_____
_____

Evening Gratitude

Date: _____   Time: _____

What caused me anxiety today?

_____

_____

_____

What did I do for myself today, and what did I say No / Yes to?

_____

_____

_____

What boundaries did I set?

_____

_____

_____

_____

My mood right now...

_____

_____

Affirmation: _____

I am grateful that today...

_____

_____

_____

_____

_____

_____

Daily Gratitude

Date: _____   Time: _____

My mood right now...
_____
_____

I am grateful for

1 _____
2 _____
3 _____

Today's Affirmation

I am _____
_____
_____
_____

I am looking forward to...
_____
_____
_____

What can I do for myself today?
_____
_____
_____

Evening Gratitude

Date: _____   Time: _____

What caused me anxiety today?

_____

_____

_____

What did I do for myself today, and what did I say No/Yes to?

_____

_____

_____

What boundaries did I set?

_____

_____

_____

_____

My mood right now...

_____

_____

Affirmation: _____

I am grateful that today...

_____

_____

_____

_____

_____

_____

Daily Gratitude

Date: _____   Time: _____

My mood right now...

_____

_____

I am grateful for

1 _____

2 _____

3 _____

Today's Affirmation

I am _____

_____

_____

_____

I am looking forward to...

_____

_____

_____

What can I do for myself today?

_____

_____

_____

_____

Evening Gratitude

Date: _____   Time: _____

What caused me anxiety today?

_____

_____

_____

What did I do for myself today, and what did I say No/ Yes to?

_____

_____

_____

What boundaries did I set?

_____

_____

_____

_____

My mood right now...

_____

_____

Affirmation: _____

I am grateful that today...

_____

_____

_____

_____

_____

_____

Daily Gratitude

Date: _____   Time: _____

My mood right now...

_____

I am grateful for

1 _____
2 _____
3 _____

Today's Affirmation

I am _____
_____
_____
_____

I am looking forward to...

_____
_____
_____

What can I do for myself today?

_____
_____
_____

Evening Gratitude

Date: _____   Time: _____

What caused me anxiety today? _____

_____

_____

What did I do for myself today,
and what did I say No/Yes to?

_____

_____

What boundaries did I set?

_____

_____

_____

My mood right now...

_____

_____

Affirmation: _____

I am grateful that today... _____

_____

_____

_____

_____

_____

Daily Gratitude

Date: _____   Time: _____

My mood right now...
_____
_____

I am grateful for

1 _____
2 _____
3 _____

Today's Affirmation

I am _____
_____
_____
_____

I am looking forward to...
_____
_____
_____

What can I do for myself today?
_____
_____
_____

Evening Gratitude

Date: _____   Time: _____

What caused me anxiety today?

_____

_____

_____

What did I do for myself today,
and what did I say No/ Yes to?

_____

_____

_____

What boundaries did I set?

_____

_____

_____

My mood right now...

_____

_____

Affirmation:

I am grateful that today...

_____

_____

_____

_____

_____

_____

Daily Gratitude

Date: _____   Time: _____

My mood right now...

_____

_____

I am grateful for

1 _____

2 _____

3 _____

Today's Affirmation

I am _____

_____

_____

_____

I am looking forward to...

_____

_____

_____

_____

What can I do for myself today?

_____

_____

_____

_____

Evening Gratitude

Date: _____   Time: _____

What caused me anxiety today?

_____

_____

_____

What did I do for myself today,
and what did I say No/Yes to?

_____

_____

What boundaries did I set?

_____

_____

_____

My mood right now...

_____

Affirmation: _____

I am grateful that today...

_____

_____

_____

_____

_____

Daily Gratitude

Date: _____   Time: _____

My mood right now...
_____
_____

I am grateful for

1 _____
2 _____
3 _____

Today's Affirmation

I am _____
_____
_____
_____

I am looking forward to...
_____
_____
_____

What can I do for myself today?
_____
_____
_____

Evening Gratitude

Date: _____   Time: _____

What caused me anxiety today?

_____

_____

_____

What did I do for myself today,
and what did I say No/Yes to?

_____

_____

What boundaries did I set?

_____

_____

_____

_____

My mood right now...

_____

_____

Affirmation:

I am grateful that today...

_____

_____

_____

_____

_____

_____

Daily Gratitude

Date: _____   Time: _____

My mood right now...

_____

_____

I am grateful for

1 _____

2 _____

3 _____

Today's Affirmation

I am _____

_____

_____

_____

I am looking forward to...

_____

_____

_____

What can I do for myself today?

_____

_____

_____

Evening Gratitude

Date: _____   Time: _____

What caused me anxiety today?

_____

_____

_____

What did I do for myself today,
and what did I say No/ Yes to?

_____

_____

What boundaries did I set?

_____

_____

_____

_____

My mood right now...

_____

_____

Affirmation:

I am grateful that today...

_____

_____

_____

_____

_____

Daily Gratitude

Date: _____   Time: _____

My mood right now...
_____
_____

I am grateful for

1 _____
2 _____
3 _____

Today's Affirmation

I am _____
_____
_____
_____

I am looking forward to...
_____
_____
_____

What can I do for myself today?
_____
_____
_____

Evening Gratitude

Date: _____   Time: _____

What caused me anxiety today?

_____

_____

_____

What did I do for myself today,
and what did I say No/Yes to?

_____

_____

What boundaries did I set?

_____

_____

_____

_____

My mood right now...

_____

_____

Affirmation:

I am grateful that today...

_____

_____

_____

_____

_____

Daily Gratitude

Date: _____   Time: _____

My mood right now...
_____
_____

I am grateful for

1 _____

2 _____

3 _____

Today's Affirmation

I am _____
_____
_____
_____

I am looking forward to...
_____
_____
_____

What can I do for myself today?
_____
_____
_____
_____

Evening Gratitude

Date: _____   Time: _____

What caused me anxiety today?

_____

_____

_____

What did I do for myself today, and what did I say No/Yes to?

_____

_____

What boundaries did I set?

_____

_____

_____

My mood right now...

_____

_____

Affirmation:

_____

I am grateful that today...

_____

_____

_____

_____

_____

_____

Daily Gratitude

Date: _____   Time: _____

My mood right now...

_____

_____

I am grateful for

1 _____

2 _____

3 _____

Today's Affirmation

I am _____

_____

_____

_____

I am looking forward to...

_____

_____

_____

What can I do for myself today?

_____

_____

_____

Evening Gratitude

Date: _____   Time: _____

What caused me anxiety today?

_____

_____

_____

What did I do for myself today,
and what did I say No/ Yes to?

_____

_____

What boundaries did I set?

_____

_____

_____

_____

My mood right now...

_____

_____

Affirmation:

I am grateful that today...

_____

_____

_____

_____

_____

Daily Gratitude

Date: _____   Time: _____

My mood right now...
_____
_____

I am grateful for

1 _____
2 _____
3 _____

Today's Affirmation

I am _____
_____
_____
_____

I am looking forward to...
_____
_____
_____

What can I do for myself today?
_____
_____
_____

Evening Gratitude

Date: _____ Time: _____

What caused me anxiety today?

_____

_____

_____

What did I do for myself today,
and what did I say No / Yes to?

_____

_____

_____

What boundaries did I set?

_____

_____

_____

_____

My mood right now...

_____

_____

Affirmation:

I am grateful that today...

_____

_____

_____

_____

_____

_____

Daily Gratitude

Date: _____   Time: _____

My mood right now...

_____

_____

I am grateful for

1 _____

2 _____

3 _____

Today's Affirmation

I am _____

_____

_____

_____

I am looking forward to...

_____

_____

_____

What can I do for myself today?

_____

_____

_____

_____

Evening Gratitude

Date: _____   Time: _____

What caused me anxiety today?

_____

_____

_____

What did I do for myself today,
and what did I say No/Yes to?

_____

_____

What boundaries did I set?

_____

_____

_____

_____

My mood right now...

_____

_____

Affirmation:

I am grateful that today...

_____

_____

_____

_____

_____

_____

Daily Gratitude

Date: _____   Time: _____

My mood right now...
_____
_____

I am grateful for

1 _____
2 _____
3 _____

Today's Affirmation

I am _____
_____
_____
_____

I am looking forward to...
_____
_____
_____

What can I do for myself today?
_____
_____
_____

Evening Gratitude

Date: _____   Time: _____

What caused me anxiety today?
_____
_____
_____

What did I do for myself today,
and what did I say No/Yes to?
_____
_____
_____

What boundaries did I set?
_____
_____
_____
_____

My mood right now...
_____
_____

Affirmation:

I am grateful that today...
_____
_____
_____
_____
_____
_____

Daily Gratitude

Date: _____ Time: _____

My mood right now...

_____

_____

I am grateful for

1 _____

2 _____

3 _____

Today's Affirmation

I am _____

_____

_____

_____

I am looking forward to...

_____

_____

_____

What can I do for myself today?

_____

_____

_____

Evening Gratitude

Date: _____   Time: _____

What caused me anxiety today?

_____

_____

_____

What did I do for myself today,
and what did I say No / Yes to?

_____

_____

What boundaries did I set?

_____

_____

_____

My mood right now...

_____

Affirmation:

I am grateful that today...

_____

_____

_____

_____

_____

Daily Gratitude

Date: _____   Time: _____

My mood right now...

_____

_____

I am grateful for

1 _____

2 _____

3 _____

Today's Affirmation

I am _____

_____

_____

_____

I am looking forward to...

_____

_____

_____

What can I do for myself today?

_____

_____

_____

Evening Gratitude

Date: _____   Time: _____

What caused me anxiety today?

_____

_____

What did I do for myself today,
and what did I say No/Yes to?

_____

_____

What boundaries did I set?

_____

_____

_____

My mood right now...

_____

_____

Affirmation:

I am grateful that today...

_____

_____

_____

_____

_____

Daily Gratitude

Date: _____

Time: _____

My mood right now...

_____

_____

I am grateful for

1 _____

2 _____

3 _____

Today's Affirmation

I am _____

_____

_____

_____

I am looking forward to...

_____

_____

_____

What can I do for myself today?

_____

_____

_____

Evening Gratitude

Date: _____

Time: _____

What caused me anxiety today?

_____

_____

_____

What did I do for myself today, and what did I say No/ Yes to?

_____

_____

_____

What boundaries did I set?

_____

_____

_____

My mood right now...

_____

_____

Affirmation:

I am grateful that today...

_____

_____

_____

_____

_____

_____

Daily Gratitude

Date: _____   Time: _____

My mood right now...
_____
_____

I am grateful for

1 _____
2 _____
3 _____

Today's Affirmation

I am _____
_____
_____
_____

I am looking forward to...
_____
_____
_____

What can I do for myself today?
_____
_____
_____

Evening Gratitude

Date: _____   Time: _____

What caused me anxiety today?

_____

_____

_____

What did I do for myself today, and what did I say No/ Yes to?

_____

_____

_____

What boundaries did I set?

_____

_____

_____

_____

My mood right now...

_____

_____

Affirmation: _____

I am grateful that today...

_____

_____

_____

_____

_____

Daily Gratitude

Date: _____   Time: _____

My mood right now...
_____
_____

I am grateful for

1 _____
2 _____
3 _____

Today's Affirmation

I am _____
_____
_____
_____

I am looking forward to...
_____
_____
_____

What can I do for myself today?
_____
_____
_____

Evening Gratitude

Date: _____   Time: _____

What caused me anxiety today?
_____
_____
_____

What did I do for myself today,
and what did I say No/Yes to?
_____
_____
_____

What boundaries did I set?
_____
_____
_____
_____

My mood right now...
_____
_____
_____

Affirmation:
_____

I am grateful that today...
_____
_____
_____
_____
_____
_____

Daily Gratitude

Date: _____   Time: _____

My mood right now...

_____

I am grateful for

1 _____

2 _____

3 _____

Today's Affirmation

I am _____

_____

_____

_____

I am looking forward to...

_____

_____

_____

What can I do for myself today?

_____

_____

_____

Evening Gratitude

Date: _____   Time: _____

What caused me anxiety today?

_____

_____

_____

What did I do for myself today, and what did I say No/ Yes to?

_____

_____

_____

What boundaries did I set?

_____

_____

_____

_____

My mood right now...

_____

_____

Affirmation:

I am grateful that today...

_____

_____

_____

_____

_____

_____

Daily Gratitude

Date: _____   Time: _____

My mood right now...

_____

I am grateful for

1 _____

2 _____

3 _____

Today's Affirmation

I am _____

_____

_____

_____

I am looking forward to...

_____

_____

_____

What can I do for myself today?

_____

_____

_____

Evening Gratitude

Date: _____ Time: _____

What caused me anxiety today?

_____

_____

_____

What did I do for myself today,
and what did I say No/Yes to?

_____

_____

_____

What boundaries did I set?

_____

_____

_____

_____

My mood right now...

_____

_____

_____

Affirmation:

I am grateful that today...

_____

_____

_____

_____

_____

_____

Daily Gratitude

Date: _____   Time: _____

My mood right now...
_____
_____

I am grateful for

1 _____
2 _____
3 _____

Today's Affirmation

I am _____
_____
_____
_____

I am looking forward to...
_____
_____
_____

What can I do for myself today?
_____
_____
_____
_____

Evening Gratitude

Date: _____   Time: _____

What caused me anxiety today?

_____

_____

_____

What did I do for myself today, and what did I say No / Yes to?

_____

_____

What boundaries did I set?

_____

_____

_____

My mood right now...

_____

_____

Affirmation:

_____

I am grateful that today...

_____

_____

_____

_____

_____

_____

Daily Gratitude

Date: _____   Time: _____

My mood right now...

_____

_____

I am grateful for

1 _____

2 _____

3 _____

Today's Affirmation

I am _____

_____

_____

_____

I am looking forward to...

_____

_____

_____

What can I do for myself today?

_____

_____

_____

Evening Gratitude

Date: _____   Time: _____

What caused me anxiety today?

_____

_____

_____

What did I do for myself today,
and what did I say No/ Yes to?

_____

_____

_____

What boundaries did I set?

_____

_____

_____

My mood right now...

_____

_____

Affirmation:

I am grateful that today...

_____

_____

_____

_____

_____

_____

Daily Gratitude

Date: _____   Time: _____

My mood right now...
_____

I am grateful for

1 _____
2 _____
3 _____

Today's Affirmation

I am _____
_____
_____
_____

I am looking forward to...
_____
_____
_____

What can I do for myself today?
_____
_____
_____

Evening Gratitude

Date: _____   Time: _____

What caused me anxiety today?

_____
_____
_____

What did I do for myself today,
and what did I say No / Yes to?

_____
_____
_____

What boundaries did I set?

_____
_____
_____
_____

My mood right now...

_____
_____

Affirmation:

I am grateful that today...

_____
_____
_____
_____
_____
_____

Daily Gratitude

Date: _____   Time: _____

My mood right now...

_____

_____

I am grateful for

1 _____

2 _____

3 _____

Today's Affirmation

I am _____

_____

_____

_____

I am looking forward to...

_____

_____

_____

What can I do for myself today?

_____

_____

_____

Evening Gratitude

Date: _____   Time: _____

What caused me anxiety today?

_____

_____

What did I do for myself today,
and what did I say No/Yes to?

_____

_____

What boundaries did I set?

_____

_____

_____

My mood right now...

_____

_____

Affirmation:

I am grateful that today...

_____

_____

_____

_____

_____

_____

Daily Gratitude

Date: _____   Time: _____

My mood right now...

_____

_____

I am grateful for

1 _____

2 _____

3 _____

Today's Affirmation

I am _____

_____

_____

_____

I am looking forward to...

_____

_____

_____

What can I do for myself today?

_____

_____

_____

Evening Gratitude

Date: _____   Time: _____

What caused me anxiety today?

_____
_____
_____

What did I do for myself today,
and what did I say No/ Yes to?

_____
_____

What boundaries did I set?

_____
_____
_____
_____

My mood right now...

_____
_____

Affirmation:

I am grateful that today...

_____
_____
_____
_____
_____

Daily Gratitude

Date: _____   Time: _____

My mood right now...

_____

I am grateful for

1 _____

2 _____

3 _____

Today's Affirmation

I am _____

_____

_____

_____

I am looking forward to...

_____

_____

_____

What can I do for myself today?

_____

_____

_____

Evening Gratitude

Date: _____   Time: _____

What caused me anxiety today? _____

_____

_____

_____

What did I do for myself today,
and what did I say No/ Yes to?

_____

_____

_____

What boundaries did I set?

_____

_____

_____

_____

My mood right now...

_____

_____

Affirmation: _____

I am grateful that today... _____

_____

_____

_____

_____

_____

_____

Daily Gratitude

Date: _____   Time: _____

My mood right now...
_____
_____

I am grateful for

1 _____
2 _____
3 _____

Today's Affirmation

I am _____
_____
_____
_____

I am looking forward to...
_____
_____
_____

What can I do for myself today?
_____
_____
_____

Evening Gratitude

Date: _____   Time: _____

What caused me anxiety today? _____
_____
_____

What did I do for myself today, and what did I say No/ Yes to?
_____
_____

What boundaries did I set?
_____
_____
_____
_____

My mood right now...
_____
_____

Affirmation: _____

I am grateful that today... _____
_____
_____
_____
_____
_____

Daily Gratitude

Date: _____   Time: _____

My mood right now...
_____
_____

I am grateful for

1 _____

2 _____

3 _____

Today's Affirmation

I am _____
_____
_____
_____

I am looking forward to...
_____
_____
_____

What can I do for myself today?
_____
_____
_____

Evening Gratitude

Date: _____   Time: _____

What caused me anxiety today?

_____

_____

What did I do for myself today,
and what did I say No/Yes to?

_____

_____

What boundaries did I set?

_____

_____

_____

My mood right now...

_____

_____

Affirmation:

I am grateful that today...

_____

_____

_____

_____

Daily Gratitude

Date: _____   Time: _____

My mood right now...
_____
_____

I am grateful for

1 _____

2 _____

3 _____

Today's Affirmation

I am _____
_____
_____
_____

I am looking forward to...
_____
_____
_____

What can I do for myself today?
_____
_____
_____
_____

Evening Gratitude

Date: _____   Time: _____

What caused me anxiety today? _____
_____
_____
_____

What did I do for myself today,
and what did I say No/Yes to?
_____
_____
_____

What boundaries did I set?
_____
_____
_____
_____

My mood right now...
_____
_____

Affirmation: _____

I am grateful that today... _____
_____
_____
_____
_____
_____

Daily Gratitude

Date: _____   Time: _____

My mood right now...
_____
_____

I am grateful for

1 _____

2 _____

3 _____

Today's Affirmation

I am _____
_____
_____
_____

I am looking forward to...
_____
_____
_____

What can I do for myself today?
_____
_____
_____

Evening Gratitude

Date: _____   Time: _____

What caused me anxiety today?

_____
_____
_____

What did I do for myself today,
and what did I say No/Yes to?

_____
_____
_____

What boundaries did I set?

_____
_____
_____
_____

My mood right now...

_____
_____

Affirmation:

I am grateful that today...

_____
_____
_____
_____
_____

Daily Gratitude

Date: _____   Time: _____

My mood right now...

_____

_____

I am grateful for

1 _____

2 _____

3 _____

Today's Affirmation

I am _____

_____

_____

_____

I am looking forward to...

_____

_____

_____

What can I do for myself today?

_____

_____

_____

Evening Gratitude

Date: _____   Time: _____

What caused me anxiety today?

_____

_____

_____

What did I do for myself today,
and what did I say No/Yes to?

_____

_____

_____

What boundaries did I set?

_____

_____

_____

_____

My mood right now...

_____

_____

_____

Affirmation:

I am grateful that today...

_____

_____

_____

_____

_____

_____

Daily Gratitude

Date: _____   Time: _____

My mood right now...
_____
_____

I am grateful for

1 _____
2 _____
3 _____

Today's Affirmation

I am _____
_____
_____
_____

I am looking forward to...
_____
_____
_____

What can I do for myself today?
_____
_____
_____

Evening Gratitude

Date: _____   Time: _____

What caused me anxiety today?

_____

_____

_____

What did I do for myself today, and what did I say No/Yes to?

_____

_____

What boundaries did I set?

_____

_____

_____

My mood right now...

_____

_____

Affirmation: _____

I am grateful that today...

_____

_____

_____

_____

_____

Daily Gratitude

Date: _____   Time: _____

My mood right now...

_____

I am grateful for

1 _____

2 _____

3 _____

Today's Affirmation

I am _____

_____

_____

_____

I am looking forward to...

_____

_____

_____

What can I do for myself today?

_____

_____

_____

Evening Gratitude

Date: _____   Time: _____

What caused me anxiety today?

_____

_____

_____

What did I do for myself today,
and what did I say No/Yes to?

_____

_____

What boundaries did I set?

_____

_____

_____

_____

My mood right now...

_____

_____

Affirmation: _____

I am grateful that today...

_____

_____

_____

_____

_____

_____

Daily Gratitude

Date: _____   Time: _____

My mood right now...
_____
_____

I am grateful for

1 _____
2 _____
3 _____

Today's Affirmation

I am _____
_____
_____
_____

I am looking forward to...
_____
_____
_____

What can I do for myself today?
_____
_____
_____
_____

Evening Gratitude

Date: _____ Time: _____

What caused me anxiety today?

_____

_____

_____

What did I do for myself today,
and what did I say No/Yes to?

_____

_____

What boundaries did I set?

_____

_____

_____

My mood right now...

_____

_____

Affirmation:

I am grateful that today...

_____

_____

_____

_____

_____

_____

Daily Gratitude

Date: _____   Time: _____

My mood right now...
_____
_____

I am grateful for

1 _____

2 _____

3 _____

Today's Affirmation

I am _____
_____
_____
_____

I am looking forward to...
_____
_____
_____

What can I do for myself today?
_____
_____
_____
_____

Evening Gratitude

Date: _____   Time: _____

What caused me anxiety today?

_____

_____

What did I do for myself today,
and what did I say No / Yes to?

_____

_____

What boundaries did I set?

_____

_____

_____

_____

My mood right now...

_____

_____

Affirmation:

I am grateful that today...

_____

_____

_____

_____

_____

Daily Gratitude

Date: _____   Time: _____

My mood right now...

_____

_____

I am grateful for

1 _____

2 _____

3 _____

Today's Affirmation

I am _____

_____

_____

_____

I am looking forward to...

_____

_____

_____

What can I do for myself today?

_____

_____

_____

Evening Gratitude

Date: _____   Time: _____

What caused me anxiety today?

_____

_____

_____

What did I do for myself today,
and what did I say No/Yes to?

_____

_____

What boundaries did I set?

_____

_____

_____

My mood right now...

_____

_____

Affirmation:

I am grateful that today...

_____

_____

_____

_____

_____

_____

Daily Gratitude

Date: _____   Time: _____

My mood right now...

_____

_____

I am grateful for

1 _____

2 _____

3 _____

Today's Affirmation

I am _____

_____

_____

_____

I am looking forward to...

_____

_____

_____

What can I do for myself today?

_____

_____

_____

Evening Gratitude

Date: _____

Time: _____

What caused me anxiety today?

_____

_____

_____

What did I do for myself today,
and what did I say No/Yes to?

_____

_____

_____

What boundaries did I set?

_____

_____

_____

_____

My mood right now...

_____

_____

_____

Affirmation: _____

I am grateful that today...

_____

_____

_____

_____

_____

_____

Daily Gratitude

Date: _____   Time: _____

My mood right now...

_____

_____

I am grateful for

1 _____

2 _____

3 _____

Today's Affirmation

I am _____

_____

_____

_____

I am looking forward to...

_____

_____

_____

What can I do for myself today?

_____

_____

_____

_____

Evening Gratitude

Date: _____   Time: _____

What caused me anxiety today? _____
_____
_____
_____

What did I do for myself today,
and what did I say No/Yes to?
_____
_____

What boundaries did I set?
_____
_____
_____

My mood right now...
_____
_____

Affirmation: _____

I am grateful that today... _____
_____
_____
_____
_____
_____

Daily Gratitude

Date: _____   Time: _____

My mood right now...
_____
_____

I am grateful for

1 _____
2 _____
3 _____

Today's Affirmation

I am _____
_____
_____
_____

I am looking forward to...
_____
_____
_____

What can I do for myself today?
_____
_____
_____

Evening Gratitude

Date: _____

Time: _____

What caused me anxiety today?

_____
_____
_____

What did I do for myself today,
and what did I say No/Yes to?

_____
_____
_____

What boundaries did I set?

_____
_____
_____
_____

My mood right now...

_____
_____

Affirmation:

I am grateful that today...

_____
_____
_____
_____
_____

Daily Gratitude

Date: _____

Time: _____

My mood right now...

_____

_____

I am grateful for

1 _____

2 _____

3 _____

Today's Affirmation

I am _____

_____

_____

_____

I am looking forward to...

_____

_____

_____

What can I do for myself today?

_____

_____

_____

Evening Gratitude

Date: _____   Time: _____

What caused me anxiety today? _____
_____
_____
_____

What did I do for myself today,
and what did I say No/ Yes to?
_____
_____
_____

What boundaries did I set?
_____
_____
_____

My mood right now...
_____
_____

Affirmation: _____

I am grateful that today... _____
_____
_____
_____
_____
_____

Daily Gratitude

Date: _____   Time: _____

My mood right now...

_____

_____

I am grateful for

1 _____

2 _____

3 _____

Today's Affirmation

I am _____

_____

_____

_____

I am looking forward to...

_____

_____

_____

What can I do for myself today?

_____

_____

_____

_____

Evening Gratitude

Date: _____   Time: _____

What caused me anxiety today?

_____
_____
_____

What did I do for myself today, and what did I say No/ Yes to?

_____
_____
_____

What boundaries did I set?

_____
_____
_____
_____

My mood right now...

_____
_____

Affirmation:

I am grateful that today...

_____
_____
_____
_____
_____
_____

Daily Gratitude

Date: _____   Time: _____

My mood right now...
_____
_____

I am grateful for

1 _____
2 _____
3 _____

Today's Affirmation

I am _____
_____
_____
_____

I am looking forward to...
_____
_____
_____

What can I do for myself today?
_____
_____
_____

Evening Gratitude

Date: _____   Time: _____

What caused me anxiety today?

_____

_____

_____

What did I do for myself today,
and what did I say No / Yes to?

_____

_____

_____

What boundaries did I set?

_____

_____

_____

_____

My mood right now...

_____

_____

_____

Affirmation:

I am grateful that today...

_____

_____

_____

_____

_____

_____

Daily Gratitude

Date: _____   Time: _____

My mood right now...

_____

_____

I am grateful for

1 _____

2 _____

3 _____

Today's Affirmation

I am _____

_____

_____

_____

I am looking forward to...

_____

_____

_____

_____

What can I do for myself today?

_____

_____

_____

Evening Gratitude

Date: _____   Time: _____

What caused me anxiety today?

_____

_____

_____

What did I do for myself today,
and what did I say No/ Yes to?

_____

_____

_____

What boundaries did I set?

_____

_____

_____

_____

My mood right now...

_____

_____

Affirmation:

_____

I am grateful that today...

_____

_____

_____

_____

_____

Daily Gratitude

Date: _____   Time: _____

My mood right now...

_____

I am grateful for

1 _____

2 _____

3 _____

Today's Affirmation

I am _____

_____

_____

_____

I am looking forward to...

_____

_____

_____

What can I do for myself today?

_____

_____

_____

Evening Gratitude

Date: _____   Time: _____

What caused me anxiety today?

_____
_____
_____

What did I do for myself today,
and what did I say No/ Yes to?

_____
_____
_____

What boundaries did I set?

_____
_____
_____
_____

My mood right now...

_____
_____

Affirmation: _____

I am grateful that today...

_____
_____
_____
_____
_____
_____

Daily Gratitude

Date: _____   Time: _____

My mood right now...
_____
_____

I am grateful for

1 _____
2 _____
3 _____

Today's Affirmation

I am _____
_____
_____
_____

I am looking forward to...
_____
_____
_____

What can I do for myself today?
_____
_____
_____

Evening Gratitude

Date: _____   Time: _____

What caused me anxiety today?

_____

_____

_____

What did I do for myself today, and what did I say No/Yes to?

_____

_____

What boundaries did I set?

_____

_____

_____

My mood right now...

_____

_____

Affirmation:

I am grateful that today...

_____

_____

_____

_____

_____

_____

_____

Daily Gratitude

Date: _____   Time: _____

My mood right now...
_____
_____

I am grateful for

1 _____

2 _____

3 _____

Today's Affirmation

I am _____
_____
_____
_____

I am looking forward to...
_____
_____
_____

What can I do for myself today?
_____
_____
_____

Evening Gratitude

Date: _____   Time: _____

What caused me anxiety today?

_____
_____
_____

What did I do for myself today,
and what did I say No/ Yes to?

_____
_____
_____

What boundaries did I set?

_____
_____
_____
_____

My mood right now...

_____
_____

Affirmation:

I am grateful that today...

_____
_____
_____
_____
_____
_____

Daily Gratitude

Date: _____   Time: _____

My mood right now...
_____
_____

I am grateful for

1 _____
2 _____
3 _____

Today's Affirmation

I am _____
_____
_____
_____

I am looking forward to...
_____
_____
_____

What can I do for myself today?
_____
_____
_____

Evening Gratitude

Date: _____

Time: _____

What caused me anxiety today?

_____

_____

_____

What did I do for myself today,
and what did I say No/Yes to?

_____

_____

What boundaries did I set?

_____

_____

_____

_____

My mood right now...

_____

_____

Affirmation:

I am grateful that today...

_____

_____

_____

_____

_____

Daily Gratitude

Date: _____   Time: _____

My mood right now...

_____

_____

I am grateful for

1 _____

2 _____

3 _____

Today's Affirmation

I am _____

_____

_____

_____

I am looking forward to...

_____

_____

_____

What can I do for myself today?

_____

_____

_____

Evening Gratitude

Date: _____   Time: _____

What caused me anxiety today?

_____
_____
_____

What did I do for myself today, and what did I say No/Yes to?

_____
_____

What boundaries did I set?

_____
_____
_____

My mood right now...

_____
_____

Affirmation:

I am grateful that today...

_____
_____
_____
_____
_____
_____

Daily Gratitude

Date: _____   Time: _____

My mood right now...
_____
_____

I am grateful for

1 _____
2 _____
3 _____

Today's Affirmation

I am _____
_____
_____
_____

I am looking forward to...
_____
_____
_____

What can I do for myself today?
_____
_____
_____

Evening Gratitude

Date: _____   Time: _____

What caused me anxiety today?

_____
_____
_____

What did I do for myself today, and what did I say No/Yes to?

_____
_____
_____

What boundaries did I set?

_____
_____
_____

My mood right now...

_____
_____

Affirmation:

I am grateful that today...

_____
_____
_____
_____
_____
_____
_____

Daily Gratitude

Date: _____   Time: _____

My mood right now...
_____
_____

I am grateful for

1 _____
2 _____
3 _____

Today's Affirmation

I am _____
_____
_____
_____

I am looking forward to...
_____
_____
_____

What can I do for myself today?
_____
_____
_____

Evening Gratitude

Date: _____   Time: _____

What caused me anxiety today?

_____

_____

_____

What did I do for myself today,
and what did I say No/Yes to?

_____

_____

_____

What boundaries did I set?

_____

_____

_____

_____

My mood right now...

_____

_____

Affirmation:

I am grateful that today...

_____

_____

_____

_____

_____

Daily Gratitude

Date: _____   Time: _____

My mood right now...
_____
_____

I am grateful for

1 _____
2 _____
3 _____

Today's Affirmation

I am _____
_____
_____
_____

I am looking forward to...
_____
_____
_____

What can I do for myself today?
_____
_____
_____

Evening Gratitude

Date: _____   Time: _____

What caused me anxiety today?

_____

_____

_____

What did I do for myself today,
and what did I say No/ Yes to?

_____

_____

_____

What boundaries did I set?

_____

_____

_____

_____

My mood right now...

_____

_____

Affirmation: _____

I am grateful that today...

_____

_____

_____

_____

_____

_____

Daily Gratitude

Date: _____   Time: _____

My mood right now...

_____

_____

I am grateful for

1 _____

2 _____

3 _____

Today's Affirmation

I am _____

_____

_____

_____

I am looking forward to...

_____

_____

_____

What can I do for myself today?

_____

_____

_____

Evening Gratitude

Date: _____   Time: _____

What caused me anxiety today?
_____
_____
_____

What did I do for myself today,
and what did I say No/ Yes to?
_____
_____
_____

What boundaries did I set?
_____
_____
_____

My mood right now...
_____
_____

Affirmation:

I am grateful that today...
_____
_____
_____
_____
_____

Daily Gratitude

Date: _____   Time: _____

My mood right now...

_____

_____

I am grateful for

1 _____

2 _____

3 _____

Today's Affirmation

I am _____

_____

_____

_____

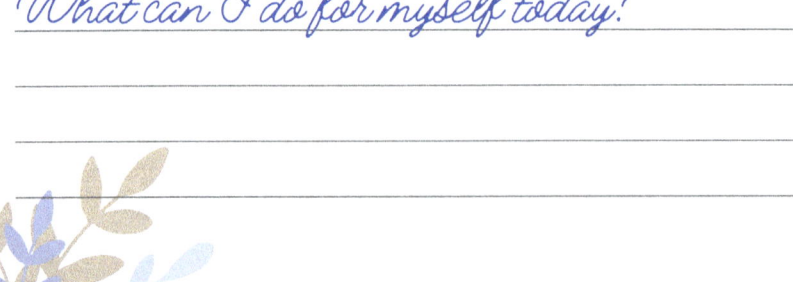

I am looking forward to...

_____

_____

_____

What can I do for myself today?

_____

_____

_____

Evening Gratitude

Date: _____   Time: _____

What caused me anxiety today?

_____

_____

What did I do for myself today,
and what did I say No/ Yes to?

_____

_____

What boundaries did I set?

_____

_____

_____

My mood right now...

_____

_____

Affirmation:

I am grateful that today...

_____

_____

_____

_____

Positive Affirmations:

1. I give myself permission to be happy with my life just as it is. Unknown
2. Everyday I am becoming a better person. Unknown
3. I will train my mind to see the good in every situation. Unknown
4. If I can stay positive in a negative situation, I win. Unknown
5. Stay positive. Better days are on their way. Unknown
6. Everyday I am becoming a better person. Unknown
7. I am valuable
8. I am worthy
9. I am good, lovable and deserve to be happy.
10. I accept me just the way I am.
11. I am a good person.
12. It's okay not to be okay.
13. I align myself only with that which serves me.
14. I am enough!
15. I am responsible for my own happiness.

Positive Affirmations:

16. I only repeat that which I want manifested.
17. I am flawed and that's ok. I am human.
18. I give myself permission to be vulnerable
19. It's my peace, I'm allowed to protect it at all cost.
20. I love and accept myself.life
21. I am beautifully and wonderfully made.
22. Purpose dwells within.
23. I inhale confidence and exhale fear.
24. I am capable
25. I give myself permission to show up as I am
26. I deserve compassion
27. I am resilient
28. I wear my scars well.
29. I will show up everyday and bring positive changes to the world around me.
30. I am grateful to have people in my

Self-Care Look Like...

Affirmations

Art

Awareness

Baths

Biking

Breathe

Candle

Canoeing

Coloring

Connections

Counseling

Crying

Cycling

Dancing

Declutter

Dining-Out

Essential Oils

Exercise

Exploration

Facials

Fire-pit

Gratitude

Hammocking

Havening

Hiking

Inspiration Board

Intimacy

Journaling

Juicing

Kayaking

Kindness

Laughter

Manicure

Massages

Meditate

Music

Napping

Nature

Painting

Pedicure

Podcast

Prayer

Prioritizing

Quiet Time

Reading

Riding

Sleep

Spa

Sun-Bathing

Therapy

Travel

Vacation

Vision Board

Walking

Yoga

Thank you. Larissa H. Rhone is a mother of two, an author, motivational speaker, sexual assault crises counselor, empowering survivors worldwide to "Reassign the Shame and Speak." As the founder of Journey 2 Free, she helps survivors turn trauma into testimony and healing into action steps. A third-generation child rape survivor, and Sickle Cell Warrior. She is passionate about purpose, motherhood, entrepreneurship, advocacy, and teaching parents and children awareness, personal body safety, healthy boundaries, and communication. She helps survivors find their voice and harness their power to live unapologetically.

Learn more at Journey2free.com

Journey 2 Free

www.ingramcontent.com/pod-product-compliance
Lightning Source LLC
Chambersburg PA
CBHW070918120626
46546CB00001B/320